Publishing

Also from Tamelia Keaton

From A Scared Life to a Loving Wife

and *Empower Publishing*

Rips, Tips and Scripts

By

Tamelia Keaton

Empower Publishing
Winston-Salem

Empower

Publishing

Empower Publishing
302 Ricks Drive
Winston-Salem, NC 27103

The opinions expressed in this work are entirely the opinions of the author and do not represent the opinions or thoughts of the publisher. The author has represented and warranted all ownership and/or legal right to publish all the materials in this book.

Copyright 2024 by Tamelia Keaton

All rights reserved, including the right of reproduction in whole or part in any format.

First Empower Publishing Books edition published
December, 2024
Empower Publishing, Feather Pen, and all production design are trademarks.

For information regarding bulk purchases of this book, digital purchase and special discounts, please contact the publisher at publish.empower.now@gmail.com

Cover design by Byron Boyce and Black Lion Multimedia.

Manufactured in the United States of America
ISBN 978-1-63066-609-5

I want to dedicate this book to every woman who is or was having thoughts that they are in this hard walk alone. This is for women who are serious about dealing with their true selves and for every mom, married or unmarried woman who needs little tips on where to start in this process. I want to also dedicate this book to every woman who may be in an abusive relationship and may not know how to get out. Last but not least, I would like to dedicate this book to my grandma Vencie Haney, who is now living in her heavenly home.

—Tamelia Keaton

Introduction/Disclosure

I am not a psychologist but a woman who has been through life and learned from my mistakes. Please use these tips to help you in your Christian walk no matter what part of it you are in. Women, this book is written to empower you, but in order to do so, you must be able to be ready to be honest with yourselves and be willing to change the behaviors so that you can get results. This is not going to be an easy road because you will have to deal with yourself which is most people's biggest enemy. Women get ready to rip the bandage off and deal with the scars so that they will heal properly. I will offer tips that can help you deal with the situation and then provide you scripts from the word of God to help you to build your foundation so that it will not keep falling down.

—Tamelia Keaton

Table of Contents

1. In the Beginning — 1
2. Any Kind of Abuse Is a No No — 7
3. Take Care of Yourself — 12
4. Get Your Finances in Order — 18
5. Deception Will Get You Nowhere — 22
6. Keep Your Enemies Close and Your Friends Closer — 26
7. Bag Ladies — 29
8. Womanhood/Motherhood — 32
9. The Alpha Wo-man — 36
10. Are You Ready to Submit? — 39
11. Are You Ready for Your Boaz or Not? — 42
12. The Married Woman — 47
13. Married Single/Single Married Woman — 50
14. A Sanctified Woman — 55

15.	The Virtuous Woman	58
16.	Give God More	62
17.	Get You a Bible-Based Church	67
18.	Iron Sharpens Iron	71

1.
In the Beginning

In Genesis, the beginning, God created man and woman for his kingdom and his creations were good. In the same book in the Bible you see the fall of man because the woman allowed herself to be tempted by the enemy and she was able to persuade her husband to follow her. This created sin and that is the reason why it is important for us to work on our inner selves as women. It is a fact, that there is at least three women to one man and I am sure this was for reproductive reasons. A man's anatomy includes an x and y chromosome and the woman's has two x chromosomes in the reproductive tract. The x's are the female hormone and the y is for the male hormone, thus proving that there are three girls to one male. This shows that women are the majority and not the minority which means if we can get ourselves together then the world can be impacted in a more positive way, which helps more than half of the world because there are far more women in the world than men. I have a desire to help women so that we can see our own self-worth not be tempted so easily by the resources of men. There is so much going on in the world that women have begun to settle for a man even if it means you are not even first, second or third in his life. A lot of this behavior comes from us not dealing with our childhood issues.

First, you must deal with your inner child. It doesn't

matter who you are, everyone has something that they have dealt with or are still dealing with from childhood that may be causing you some heartache or pain. Childhood can be the root of not being able to flourish to the beautiful woman that God created you to be. What cards have you been dealt? Your cards may have been dealt with not having a father, mother or both, rape, abuse, poverty, neglect, loneliness or even hanging around wrong influences. The cards are not the issues, the way you play the game is the key. God can still love you through all of it. There is nothing too hard for God! Sigmond Freud, a well-known psychologist, believed that childhood experiences determines how you will grow up and deal with reality. If you look back at your own self, you will probably see that part of this is true. Ladies admit it. We are products of being fatherless daughters. According to the American First Policy Institute, "approximately 18.4 million children in the U.S. live without a biological father, stepfather, or adoptive father present in the home (Brewer, Jack, 2023)." This proves that not having a father could put you at a higher risk of not being able to perform your best as an adult. This is not good because the father should set the tone of the household. The father is the man who should show his daughter what a good man looks like. He should be the first good example of what a Godsent man looks like in her life. The way a daughter sees her father treat her mother is the first example of what a real relationship should be. A father should be the first man to validate his daughter at home. A little girl is looking for her father's love, validation and protection. If the father can be that man that he was called to be, the daughter will learn the behaviors of what her worth is at a young age which helps her with what she wants her husband to look like when she is older enough in life. Not getting a father's validation from home increases the chances for the girl to look for the wrong type of validation from men in the world. It is the same for rape and abuse. Not getting the proper help for these situations can be detrimental to you in your adult life. Rape happens and most rape happens from someone that the person may know. It is time out on not bringing these skeletons out of the closet so that you can heal. Ladies, it was not your fault, and the person who did the rape should be punished. Sometimes as rape victims, we have the tendency to try to bury these skeletons deep in our hearts and hope that they don't resurface later in life. The problem with this is they are still there and just waiting for the right opportunity to resurface. We need to be delivered from these skeletons so that we can totally heal, forgive and live. Not getting these issues corrected leads to a hurt person wanting to hurt people. It is not easy but you should get counseling and not allow these situations to strangle the purpose that God has for you. Because we are not able to face our childhood issues, we risk the chances of allowing the enemy to have power over us and it has caused a lot of women to be ignorant to the word of God. We as women have decided that we want to be loved so we have become ignorant to think that we can find our own husbands based on what we want. The word says, "He who finds a wife finds a good thing, and obtains favor from the Lord (Proverbs 18:22)." **(Rip) We need to stop trying to be the flavor**

and wait so you can be the favor. (Tip) Stop looking for a man to fulfill your void of a father as a child!! Giving these men sex is not helping your purpose it only defiles the temple that we should be having clean so that God can live in us. So when you think you know what man you want and you go looking for him you will find the counterfeit man who only wants to break your heart and add to the problems that you already have. The Bible also says, "When I was a child, I spake as a child, I understood as a child: but when I became a man, I put away childish things (1 Corinthians 13:11)." Ladies, that scripture is not just for man it is for you too. **(Rip) We expect God to give us adult things when we only want to live our childlike dreams.** We have too many children running around here trying to be adults and adding hurt to the vessel. We as women need to start realizing that the Bible is not just a decorative book that goes on your living room table but it is the answer to every question or issue you are having in your own lives. We should want a closer relationship with the Lord who is the one who created us and know and love us better than we love ourselves. Stand on the word and get it down in your spirit. Jesus said, "you did not choose me, I chose you, and appointed you that you should go and bear fruit, and that your fruit should remain, that whatever you ask the father in my name he may give you (John 15:16)." Ladies we have to be the example for our young women and show them what a Godly woman looks like. **(Rip) You can't look like a Godly woman if you don't read the word to know what a Godly woman looks like!** So while you are out acting like children, **(Tip) let's**

try growing up and stepping into our rightful roles as women of God. We must understand that our ministry is not to stay in the same spot. We have to learn and grow so that we can move out the way so that people who are assigned to you by God can get the help they need from you so that they can come into Christ and you can be elevated and not stagnated. Being stagnant is a sin because God never intended for us to stay in the same spot and not grow. If you stay where you are, you could be possibly in the way of others reaching their purpose in the body of Christ. Let's grow up and be mature in Christ and stop acting like babies in the body of Christ.

Reflection: What is holding you back in your childhood that is causing you as an adult to be misunderstood?

_____
_____
_____
_____
_____
_____
_____
_____
_____
_____
_____
_____

2.
Any Kind of Abuse Is a No No

I wanted to talk about this because it has gotten way out of control because we have given the enemy too much power. **(Rip) If you or your spouse want to participate in bringing others in the bedroom sexually this is not of God it is also a form of sexual abuse!** Think about it, you should be all he needs sexually and if he allows others into your sacred place and you agree, you have given him a way to openly cheat on you. Once your relationship moves from 2 to 3 you have broken the covenant with Christ. He never put a group of people together. This is confusion which comes from Satan. The word says, "nevertheless, because of sexual immorality, let each man have his own wife and let each woman have her own husband (1 Cor. 7:2)." **(Tip) If a man thinks that you are his punching bag rather than his lady he has to go!** Men are physically stronger than women because that is the way God made it because the man is the one who works and supports. There are too many women who need to be educated on what abuse is. Abuse is anything that causes you physical, mental, sexual or emotional harm. Ladies abuse can be words, name calling, self-harm or bringing physical harm to someone else. Ladies you can be the victim or the person who is doing the harm to someone else. **(Tip) Abuse is abuse and shouldn't be welcome in your temple of God.** It may start with him raising his voice at you and embarrassing you in front of his friends. This will eventually lead to excuses, blaming it on other gods like alcohol, drugs or him not meaning to do it but it will only lead to him pushing or punching you and claiming that it will not happen again. Ladies, if you don't take a stand when it starts it can and will lead to him constantly hitting you and maybe even harming your children's feelings and causing them to have to deal with it in their adulthood. Domestic violence is real and there have been so many women that have lost their lives behind making excuses for the men and not choosing to love themselves more than that man. If you are being abused, please reach out to someone even if it is in secret. God always gives us a way of escape so whatever you need to do to get out of the situation you should do that because it could be a matter of life and death. God has given us wisdom and you know when you need to leave the situation. Do it for your children if you have them. Children didn't ask to be here therefore if you are a mother you have to make the right decisions in your life to protect your children. **(Rip) Stop putting your kids in uncompromising situations with your mess because you went looking for your own man! (Tip) Ladies, you cannot just bring anyone around your children and you don't even know them well.** These days you have pedophiles that only want to date you because of your children and now you put your children at risk of being raped, sexually abused or even physically abused. Women, we have to stand up because God didn't give us a spirit of fear, so we need to get out of these situations and utilize the law if need be. Take a stand to show them that they don't control anything and that they are not what God has for you. **(Rip) Ladies, if you call the law, keep the law!** Don't take out these restraining orders then drop them because you think he's better. **(Tip) If he didn't find God and went to get some real help he is not better.** He is just the same man who will hit you again but now he knows what to say or do to make you trust him over God. Most of the men who beat on women are nothing but men who want control because they need to deal with the inner child in themselves. Too many women have died by the hands of their boyfriends or husbands which mean we were not smart not to marry the man knowing that he was already controlling and showing signs of abuse. Ladies run fast because allowing this type of behavior in your life will smother your purpose, ruin your self-worth, find yourself telling lies after lies to justify his negative behavior and leave you with picking up the pieces to your confused lifestyle of blaming yourself for his mistakes. Anyone whether you are male or female who gets satisfaction out of seeing someone else suffer, you need some major help! Take the first step to admit you need help and that only God can deliver you from those demons. It is ok to get some psychological help so that you can recognize that your lifestyle needs to change and that you cannot fulfill your purpose holding on to old demons. Reach out and talk in private when safe to do so. It should be about your soul getting to heaven, so if that means getting professional help, involving the law or running away as soon as possible then so be it. Don't let your life be chosen to be ended before the Creator. On the other hand, don't let your life be ended before getting it right with the Lord. If you are reading right now then it is not too late. Get help and get out so you have the opportunity to stop being controlled by your current circumstances.

Reflections: Were you the giver or receiver of any abuse; What can you do to learn and refuse to be Abused?

3.
Take Care of Yourself

As women, we have to take care of our entire selves. This is our spiritual, physical and emotional selves. **(Rip) We are overworking in the physical but underworking in the body of Christ! (Tip) We should be using the Bible to follow the examples of a what made the lady in the Bible a virtuous woman (Proverbs 10:10-31).**

(Rip) Stop lying to yourself that you are a virtuous woman but you really have a Jezebel spirit! (Tip) If you just got mad then keep reading so that you can learn how to become a virtuous woman and get delivered from being Jezebel. (Rip) If you think that the qualities that God has given us as women was meant to be used to get what you want then you are mistaken! The saying, "use what you got to get what you want" does not include giving your body to another to gain benefits for your flesh. The only thing it's going to get you is a quick lay, a bay and a short stay. Jezebel was a harlot who was out for power in the body of Christ. Jezebel is not a certain gender meaning this spirit hangs in the church and may be waiting to see where God is taking you spiritually. The power God has given you and what your purpose is to edify the body of Christ, Jezebel wants it. She or he thinks that they can have what they want and know how to play on where you are weak to get it. Men will take what you give them and move on to the next woman he can use and abuse. Now you are the one left out of the will of God because you may have been fornicating, which may have led to having babies out of wedlock and blaming every man for your past mistakes. There is a reason why God wanted man and woman to wait until they were married to be sexually active with one another. **(Tip) There are other ways to get to know someone which don't have to involve sex.** Sex confuses things and spirits become attached when they shouldn't be. The word says, "There's more to sex than mere skin on skin. Sex is as much spiritual mystery as physical fact. As written in scripture, "The two become one (1 Corinthians 6:16)." Please read the rest so that you can really see that every time you lay with a man and give that part to him you are taking on that spirit and joining with him. We should think about this and realize that we take on those spirits even when we break up with them. Why do you think it is so hard to break away from something that you know is not good for you? While you are just trying to satisfy your flesh for a minute you are killing your spirit for a lifetime! We have to stop killing our purpose and visions for a one-night stand that wasn't even good in the first place. You don't want to even see him again but now you have a spirit that you have to get rid of. We have to learn from our mistakes and take our rightful place. We are much more than a man's one-night stand, a quick fix for him to use to help abuse another woman. Women, we need to have morals and values and realize that we can control the ballgame. Waiting on God and waiting to be intimate with a man until marriage will show that man that you love yourself and that you are not settling for false love called sex but you are waiting for God's love called intimacy. God can do anything but fail so what he has for you is for you. **(Tip) ladies, stop being down with the o-p-p (other people's property) and get real about the G-o-d.** The Bible says, "But seek ye first the kingdom of God, and his righteousness; and all these things shall be added unto you (Matthew 6:33)." The principles have to be done in order. Seek first and then all will be added. This is everything that you are praying for. If you want a husband use this scripture in everything you do so things will open up right for you. There are things you need to do before you are ready for a Godly man. You have to get yourself right first.

(Rip) Stop looking for a man to support and make you better when God has already made you fearfully and wonderfully made! **(Tip) A Godly man only complements who you are already in Christ.** The Bible says, "I will praise thee; for I am fearfully and wonderfully made; marvelous are thy works; and that my soul knoweth right well (Psalms 139:14)." Women, we got to know the tricks of the enemy. Remember that the enemy has no power unless you give it to him. He will tell you what you want to hear just to get what he wants. Whatever he is telling you that is making you weak for him, is where you need to put your focus to correct it so that it will not cause you to be weak in your flesh. Again deal with your spirit being first so that you can learn to die to flesh and recognize the spirit. Then you need to deal with your mental self by motivating and validating your mind with the word of God. It is impossible for a man to build your self-esteem. Self-esteem comes within your own self and how you feel about you. You have to validate yourself with God's words and stand on scriptures that will motivate and help you build yourself. The word says, "For I know the thoughts that I think toward you, saith the Lord, thoughts of peace, and not of evil, to give you an expected end (Jeremiah 29:11)." We have to get our emotional selves in check. **(Tip) God doesn't care about our emotions and neither does a worldly man.** Most men have three emotions; happy, mad and about to be mad while women have a lot of emotions. Woman was created different than man so that it would be a balance. **(Rip) While you are all into him and want to support and give him all of you he have no earthly idea of how to do the same thing for you. (Tip) Man has to learn love from God because the worldly man only know lust.** His love is what you look like and what you can do for him, so now that the cat is out of the bag how can you use this to help your whole self? The Bible also says, "My people are destroyed for lack of knowledge: because thou hast rejected knowledge, I will also reject thee, that thou shalt be no priest to me: seeing thou hast forgotten the law of thy God, I will also forget thy children (Hosea 4:6)." We cannot continue to be ignorant when we know better. You have to take the word of God and apply it to your life. Again I tell you that this is not an easy task to work on the person you see in the mirror. If you don't like what you see God has given you the scripts to change it. If it's your weight, your health that is making your self-esteem low then you must do positive things to get it right. You may need to change your diet, exercise more or even deal with your stress in a better way. **(Tip) No man wants a broken woman who doesn't love their own self and he has to tell them lies so he can get what he want to satisfy himself.** Most men love a challenge and don't like something that they can conquer in a week. **(Rip) Don't make yourself be the bet in the locker room or the top of the conversation in the men's bathroom. (Tip) Don't be that bet or that challenge however be a part of the conversation with those who means the most to him.** Your physical is also important. An attraction is the first step of a man wanting to look your way. It may start off as a physical from the eye which may include your looks, body appearance or your attitude. **(Rip) You can be the best look on the outside but your inside can still be jacked up! (Tip) Men are very smart and not just the first ones made for a reason.** Men have the ability to find out that you are insecure, broken and easy for you to give them what they want. That gives them control and it will not take much for them to satisfy you and another too. We again have to put God first, know our worth so we will not get hurt. Deny your flesh and be strong in the spirit and set the tone on what you are looking for in a man and that you will not settle for his antics.

Reflections: What positive ways will you adopt to help you stay on the top?

_____

_____

_____

4.
Get Your Finances in Order

Taking care of yourself also includes your financial health and your credit. Depending on your age, while growing up our grandparents and parents may have not taught us a lot on credit and managing our finances but it is so important. We have to be smart about getting the knowledge to learn ways that we can be financially successful. You can sign up for classes or go and see your local banker on ways that you can build your credit. **(Rip) Just because you have a little money buried in your backyard or under your mattress doesn't make you credit worthy on purchasing a piece of property!** **(Tip) You have to be able to show that you are responsible with your money, your bills are paid on time and that you have a good credit score to back it up.** If you are one of those women who has all your bills in somebody's name or even in your children's name you need to change this. You should be able to stand on your own and if you can't buy it on your own then God must not want you to have it right now. We should be able to manage our spending habits and start saving money for a rainy day. Stop trying to keep up with the Joneses and stay in the lane God has you in. We must stop getting in crazy men situations because you feel you need help with the finances. A man shouldn't be your support you should be his benefit. You should be already financially secure in yours so when your man comes, you guys can experience overflow together. You do this by honoring what the Bible says about paying your tithes and offerings. The word says, "Will a man rob God? Yet ye have robbed thee? In tithes and offerings. Ye are cursed with a curse: for ye have robbed me, even this whole nation (Malachi 3:8-9)." If you read further it states that "You are cursed with a curse but if you do right he will rebuke the devourer for your sake and open up the windows of heaven and pour you out a blessing that you won't have room to receive it (Malachi 3:10-11)." So again we now have the knowledge so how will you use it? Why are you wanting a man to do what God has already said he would do for you? **(Rip) When you don't pay your tithes you are cursed with a curse so why feel that God should bless you with the best of the best?** You think that you have it all together, you work a good job, driving a nice ride and live in a nice house to try to find what you think is a good man. **(Rip) You need to stop flaunting in your goods for God when you know God didn't give you the goods.** They are not even yours they are stolen goods, because you are not being faithful in paying your tithes and offerings.

You are still cursed with the curse and you are struggling to make the rent or car payment and you think you need a man to help you keep the stolen goods. Then you have the nerve to claim that God gave you everything when you gave God nothing. **(Tip) You must work the principle in order meaning you should pay your tithes which is ten percent from the top and offer an offering of your income.** The ten percent is required from God but your offerings is you trusting God. We should be honored to have an opportunity to believe his word and to trust God on his words. Once you work the principle right you will realize that you have to do less in trying to rob Peter to pay Paul. You will also show God that you are faithful with the little and that he can trust you with more. The Bible speaks of getting knowledge, wisdom and understanding therefore we must know, be wise and understand that God will give us the desires of our heart only when it lines up with his will. So now that we have the wisdom let's pray to our spiritual father and ask him what can you do to help his will be done? I like it when people say, "I do what I can do when I can do it!" But my saying is, "Stop doing what you do so He can do it!" God can do everything, but we don't let him work in our lives. Let's try Jesus in everything in our lives.

Reflections: How will you learn to manage your purse by paying your tithes and offering first so you are not cursed with a curse?

_____

_____

_____

_____

_____

_____

_____

_____

_____

5.
Deception Will Get You Nowhere

It is time that you stop trying to be someone else because you are not happy with yourself. **(Rip) Stop lying to yourself about who you are and what you got and don't need!** Men know the type woman who proclaims that she has it all together and don't need him for nothing. You got a long track record of being with men and still haven't got your Godsent man yet. This is because you are not ready and you don't even know who you are in Christ. **(Rip) Now how can Christ send you the right man when you are the wrong person?!** We must be true with ourselves. Admit that we have made some bad decisions or missed the mark a couple of times. There is no perfect person under the sun and if God can accept who you are with all your flaws, a man can do the same. You have been using deception, lies and half-truths to show the man that you are the person he needs in his life when really you are broke, broken and disgusted with your own self and your self-esteem is low from the previous man. **(Tip) When you stop telling yourself that you have it all together and start dealing with the woman in the mirror you will realize that you are not ready for your man of God.** Deception is anything that is not the full truth. We also need to stop telling lies to the men in our lives because it is not helping you, but it is hurting you. It is funny how you can build and uplift a man, but you are not able to build your own self-esteem. We have to get our priorities in order and know that, if we can't help ourselves, we can't be a helpmate to a man of God. Tell the truth about yourself. If he is the right man he will appreciate you telling him than he has to find out from the neighborhood. **(Rip) No man wants to think that he is getting his Godsent woman only to find out that he is getting the whole neighborhood's leftovers!** This is why it is important that you wait until you are married to give what you have to your earthly king. We learned earlier in the book that sex only complicate things and cause your flesh to rise and now you let your guard down to keep the feelings which most of the time leads to regret, abuse and an attachment that you don't want to keep. **(Tip) Remember that God wants more than an affair with you, he wants a relationship.** He needs more than church on Sunday and maybe Bible study on Wednesday. When you are in relationship you talk to that person daily, you care when you hurt him and you give more to make it right. You realize that you are not able to live without that person and let him in on every part of your life. God needs to be in the center and your daily life activities should be centered around him. God accepts you just like you are so there is no need to have to deceive others that come into your life. You can't deceive God because he sees and knows it all, so if you are living your life hiding behind a clone it will eventually stop working. The Bible mentions that he will bring it to the light and now the whole relationship was built on the wrong foundation which was deception. Ladies, just be honest with God, yourself and the people who come into your life. A real man wants to see you at your worst and your best. Stop trying to be someone else and just be yourself.

Reflections: Are you a deceiver or are you a deceiver believer?

6.
Keep Your Enemies Close And Your Friends Closer

Ladies, we are the individuals who desire friends so that your girlfriends can help you get through the rough times, but we cannot count God out. We should be talking to him just as much as we talk to our friends. Your so-called friends are people that you trust but they only want to help the enemy destroy you. Stop giving your enemies the tools they need to bring you down. You tell them everything about your relationship then you catch them with your man. Thank God for the friends that I have, and how they protect me and not try to harm me. It made me want to talk about the young girl from North Carolina who was killed in Mexico by her so-called friends and they haven't even been charged yet. Some of the story was saying these friends were envious of her and wanted what she had and they killed her and robbed her. With friends like these, who needs enemies? We've got to stop calling everyone our friends, so let me help you make better judgment on your friends. If they call all the time with what is going on with them because they are always in the same situation, be aware. You are not a trash can but you are a child of God. Don't let your so-called friends dump their trash on you and cause you to be in drama with them because they are miserable. The saying is right, misery loves company. Be aware that when God blesses you with a mate those friends always say that he is coming in between your friendship with them. This could be another trap from the enemy and that friend may want to be more than a friend. If your friend doesn't have a relationship with the same God that you do and she can't get a prayer to the one above on your behalf, you may want to consider these things when you are calling them friends. Friends support you, don't judge you and know how to pray to help you when times are bad. Friends are closer than your family and want to see the best for you. Your friend should care about where your soul will end up and should be honest enough to tell you the truth about everything out of love for you. Ladies, I know that some of us have male friends who we trust. I don't see a problem with it unless you are making it one. A male friend should be a friend and not one that you also sleep with. If you are in a relationship, your partner should also be friends with your male friends. It shouldn't cause issues in your relationship. Sometimes having an opposite sex friendship can get messy. Be careful still trying to befriend your ex-boyfriend because it is not a such thing called a male friend with benefits when you are in a relationship. This is called a disaster. This will cause division in a real relationship. Get this fix before your husband finds you. When you get in your relationship, both of you need to know all friends. Y'all friends become our friends so there should never be any secrets about who your friends are.

Reflections: How will you seek God to give you discernment on your friends and if their your enemies how will you bring it to an end?

7.
Bag Ladies

There are so many things that women like to have, and two of these things are pocketbooks and shoes. Men always say women love to shop, buy pocketbooks and shoes but that is not the bags I am talking about. I'm talking about the hidden bags inside us that the men can't help us carry. These are the things we haven't dealt with from our childhood, previous relationships and maybe just unforgiveness that you have not let go. Women are emotional and we have the tendency to nourish and hold on to bad relationships. This is why it is very important to deal with issues before meeting who God has for us. **(Rip) They are called issues for a reason because ladies (it's you).** It's nobody else's problem because you have to deal with it. I know that they hurt you but if we would have been strong in the Lord it wouldn't have happened. You don't want to run your good man away blaming him for all the problems from your previous relationships. You allowed control in the past with the fleshly man and now the man of the spirit is trying to lead you to do it his way and you are ready to quit, fight and run. **(Tip) Talk to your Father above, and use your discernment to ensure this is the right thing to do and allow that man to take the lead.** Sometimes when God makes us uncomfortable that is when we should trust God more. Together focus on putting God first in everything that both of you do and this is the first step of letting one of those bags go and moving towards freedom. Carrying too many bags will cause you to be left. You must recognize the bag, face it and leave it behind so you can move forward. Leaving bad bags behind leaves room for gaining good grounds for God which will benefit the relationship in the end because he should be the foundation that any relationship or marriage should stand on. Carry a bag with the right things in it. Carry the word of God, the real love of God and the fruits of the spirit with you at all times. Remember that "The Lord himself goes before you and will be with you; he will never leave you nor forsake you. Do not be afraid; do not be discouraged (Deuteronomy 31:8)." Ladies, I am proud of you that you have read this far and didn't give up. Again I say it is not an easy task when you have to deal with the real you instead of the fake you. Some of us have been a different person for too long that you have gotten rid of the person that God made in the beginning. God wants us to be better and I am so passionate about helping all women do better. I believe that if we can work on ourselves and know our true worth in the kingdom God will send us our helpmate so that the kingdom can be edified even more. We carry so many extra bags that we lose focus on where we are going and what we need to do next. The bags are heavy after you carry them a while, therefore they will put stress on our bodies, minds and spirits. God can't give you the good because we are too preoccupied on carrying the bags that aren't for us. We have to give the old bags to Christ and trust that he will carry them for us. Stop picking them back up!

Reflections: How will you eliminate those old bags which was hurt, disappointment and never hads?

_____
_____
_____
_____
_____
_____
_____
_____
_____
_____
_____
_____
_____
_____
_____
_____
_____
_____
_____
_____
_____

8.
Womanhood/Motherhood

It takes a lot to be a woman or mother and only we can do that best. God made woman and then said that human beings should be fruitful and multiply which means we are mothers as well. Another reason we have to be strong women is because we have our generation of girls and young ladies watching us. We as mothers don't understand that when we are not being the woman that God called us to be our children watch and pick up these bad characteristics. Generational curses are created if we are accepting all the negative things the man gives us and we don't make a stand to be who God called us to be. Our children model us when sometimes we know that we are not being the best models. Teen pregnancy, domestic abuse, deception and lies come from what we started and now it is happening with our kids. **(Rip) Stop telling your children to do what I say and not what I do!** You are saying that I am a hypocrite because I am not living the life I want you to live.

We should be better examples so the children can live as we say and do. Children are weaker but wiser and will question your authority and now you are upset. The times are different where if you are not having open conversations with your children then they will google it or get it from the streets meaning you need to be in your word so that we can honor what the Bible says, "Train up a child in the way he should go, and even when he is old he will not depart from it (Proverbs 22:6)." In order for you to do this effectively you must be the example so that our girls can have a good role model. You should watch the way you dress and look, what you say and who you are around. You can't allow yourself to make decisions to keep a man when you know they are hurting your children. Some of the decisions that you make just to be in a relationship hurts the child in the end and leads them down a path to being hurt by the same type men in their future. If you are a single mother trying to raise a son, you should be allowing a good God man to help put the qualities he needs to become a God man. Don't let your son see you being disrespected by a man because that could make him not respect women when he becomes a man. Every decision we have to make will have a consequence whether it is good or bad. Just because you are a single mother doesn't mean God will not send you a Godsent man to help you with your children. **(Rip) Ladies, stop staying with these baby daddies who don't want to stay with you; better yet stop having the babies to try to trap the man!**

He is not going to stay with you just because you're pregnant. He is moving on to the next baby momma if he hasn't already. We need to be praying and waiting and making sure you know the person that you want your children to be raised by. Genes are real and they do travel from their fathers to your children. Now you are left being a single mom and raising a child on your own because your intention was to trap him which is another form of deception. Now you mad at the child because you can't get the man! The child didn't ask to be here, you wanted the child, so now you must reap what you sowed. Now you are upset because your kids have the same qualities as their daddy and you have to deal with them alone. **(Tip) God is so good that he still allows the child to be a blessing to us anyways.** God is a just God who gives the child to us to help the child find their own purpose in helping to edify the body of Christ. Though our intentions were wrong. God is so worthy of all the praise not because of what he does but because of who he is in our own personal lives! So thank God for our challenges we've been through so far, because it is empowering us to our purpose.

Reflections: What will you put in place for your sons so that they are not dependent on you to make all of their runs? Or what do you need to change about you to show your daughter the right thing to do?

_____
_____
_____
_____
_____
_____
_____
_____
_____
_____
_____

9.
The Alpha Wo-man

I will touch a little on this subject but not much because it is out of order. Everything that happens it is because it stems from the word of God. When Eve was tempted by the enemy she in turn gives the forbidden fruit to Adam. Adam ate it and now we have men who allows their women to be in charge of them. God made man over the woman because we as women messed that up by being the weaker being and allowing the devil to tempt us. I know that some women think that they are the alpha wo-man. These are women who feel they are too strong to submit to the male. Some qualities might be they are the breadwinners and are ok with men who stay at home and not work, they are bossy, not willing to take advice from their men, always think that they are right and can't be taught anything. If you are this controlling then you need to start at the beginning to find out what happened that you need to have all the control. Submitting to your Godly man doesn't make you weak, it makes God strong. When you realize that as a woman your place is beside your man so that both of you can submit to God together your relationship will work out like it supposed to. The Bible says, "Wives submit yourselves unto your own husbands, as unto the Lord. For the husband is the head of the wife, even as Christ is the head of the church: and he is the savior of the body (Ephesians 5:22-23)." Remember ladies our job is to be a helpmate meaning you should let your husband make the final decision whether it is right or wrong. If it is the wrong decision your husband will have to deal with God but we as wives will still be covered. If God had meant for women to be alphas then he would have made us first and created the man from our rib. Women were the reason for the fall of man means that the enemy knew we would react on our emotions and we would be easily tempted. Godly men don't want alpha wo-men. They want a woman who acts and responds like a woman. If he wanted a man he would have dated one so therefore, be the being that God called you all to be which is a woman and not an alpha wo-man. Let's take our rightful place and realize that men need women just as much as we need them. In order for a relationship to work the way it intended to work both have to play their role and play it to the fullness of God and his purpose for the relationship in the beginning. A woman should walk beside a man and not in front, behind or on top of him. Women shouldn't find ways to bring a man down to make us better. You should honor him as a man and respect him especially around others.

Reflections: What challenges will you have to face to always stay in a woman's place?

_____
_____
_____
_____

10.
Are You Ready to Submit?

In order to submit you must understand what submit means. Submit is to yield to a being or a higher force. You have to be willing to be able to let someone in to help make you better and be willing to accept constructive criticism to get better. Ladies this doesn't mean that if you submit then you are not strong. It simply means that you are admitting that you need some help in getting to the best Godly you there is. The problem is we are willing to submit to the wrong individuals who take advantage of our goods to help them get their goods. Why is it that we can tell the wrong man yes and follow him to hell and back but we are not able to tell God yes so that he can show us how to get to heaven? **(Rip) How are you going to be able to submit to a Godly man and you can't even submit to the God who made the Godly man? (Tip) We have to understand that when we are in Christ, submission doesn't make us as women weak, it makes us strong.** Submitting to God allows us to let God take the reign of our lives and we're able to trust and follow him wherever he needs us to go. We have to be able to say yes to what God wants for our lives even when it doesn't make sense. We have to be willing to walk by faith even when you don't see it. Not until you submit to God, that you are able to trust your Godly man while he trusts in the God you serve. As a woman it is our role to be the helpmate. Our role is to always respect our man, hold him accountable for his actions and to keep him on the right track with God so that the entire household can be blessed. Women, I know that we are strong, independent and don't need no man to do anything for us, but on the other hand, we do want a man for support, and to help bring out the Godly woman that God has created. **(Rip) Stop saying you don't want a man because if that was true then we wouldn't be so weak to them and allow them to treat us like dogs and to devalue our worth!** We have even allowed the enemy to change our character and date women because men have hurt us so bad. **(Tip) Men shouldn't be able to change what God has done for us.** This is why we must get back to God first so that everything else will fall in order with God's will for us. You have to first submit to God and then he teaches you how to submit to your Godly man when the time comes. Part of submitting is admitting that we are not in charge but have been omitting the truth of not being in charge. We keep doing it wrong and the same way, but expecting better when it equals insanity. In order to get different results, you must do different behaviors. We have been doing it our way each time, so why not try it God's way one time?

Reflections: what is your definition of submit and how will you do it for God more so he can get you mentally fit?

11.
Are You Ready for Your Boaz or Not?

(Rip) God is not going to send you a good man when you are a good mess! (Tip) God first has to fix your good mess before he sends his Godly man. If you can't communicate which is praying to God, then you are not going to know how to communicate with any man. Communication is an essential part of any relationship. There will always be disagreements or misunderstandings in the parties. Ladies, we can't expect a Godly man to want to put up with our tantrums and insecurities all the time! You must grow up and accept that you are insecure. Insecurities come from the inside of you and can cause you to ruin something that may be good for you. This may show that you are not ready for a Godly man because you are not whole in God and yourself, which will only welcome the weak man who are the ones who need you to be his momma and not his wife. Know the weak man's qualities and attributes: they can't keep a job or they change jobs often, they are selfish with you and mad when you are not with them all the time, they want you to buy everything because they have nothing, intimidation is their game and you can't make more than they can which is not much at all; and to top it off they want to be in control and try to bring your self-worth down because they have none of their own. My Pastor and sisters at New Life will say that a man needs his own table and chairs before sitting at yours. Be careful of the man who is always in between jobs, living with family or friends and always need a ride from you. Why have the women settled with the modern day scrubs? TLC described them but women have learned to empower them. **(Tip) Remember, you are waiting on a Godsent man and not an older son who needs his mother's help.** We have all experienced at least one of them who when you're ready to break things off they're stalking because they need you. If you keep attracting this type of man you need to start back at the beginning and find out why your inner child wants to help this child called a half man. You can't change the man only God can. **(Rip) How can you as a woman change a man when you were created from the man**? We all hear it. Girl, he's going to be ok, I can change him with what I am giving him. **(Tip) It is not your job to change or raise a man it was his father's job.** Even as a single mother with a son, you can show that boy love and what a Godly woman looks like in you. You cannot help that boy become a man that is a real man's job. So whether it is his father, your father, his uncle or his Godly men in church you need to stay in a mother's place and let your son learn from a real Godly man. **(Rip) We are the reason that these momma boys exists because we baby and nurture them too long and don't know when to let them step up to learn to be a man!** Instead we give them everything they need and don't put any real principles in them so they never leave your house. Some have even taken the woman's role and they now think they are better women than you are. **(Tip) We need to go back to the principles and**

stop ignoring the fact that God made Adam and Eve and not Adam and Steve or Madam and Eve. Please read Genesis chapter 2 so that you can also see that when you get married that man is "to leave his mother and father, and shall cleave unto his wife: and they shall be one flesh (Gen 2:24)." We as mothers have to let our sons go and shouldn't allow our sons to put us in the middle of their relationships. This might be in order for man but out of order for God. If you are a single mother with a son and you are asking God to send you a Boaz then you can't allow your son to get in the way of what God has for you. We can't expect for God to give us everything when we gave God nothing. God wants to know that he can trust us first and that we will honor him and give him the praise that is due to him. **(Rip) God can't give you a Godly man if you yourself are not Godly!**

If you are not saved and trying to live a God life then you will only understand the unsaved man who can only offer you lust and not love. **(Tip) When you get saved, sanctified and filled with the Holy Spirit then you will attract Godly men of the same spirit.** Women, it is ignorant to think that you are going to get the perfect man when you don't know what God's perfection looks like! In order to know what a Godly man looks like you have to be close to God and get in the word of God. Humans think that marriage is a good thing but it is a God thing. The Bible speaks of marriages and how important it is in God's eyes. Ladies, vows are real and should be taken seriously. The word speaks how two is better than one and in a marriage you should cover one another. What are you willing to give up to make your marriage good in God's eyes? You can't get tired of him and have something on the side when it doesn't work anymore and not be willing to stand by him when his physical health is not the same when you married him. You cannot marry a man because he looks good, can lay it down right or he has all the money in the world. Material things will fade away. His looks can change, his performance will need some help and his money can run out meaning you better have the right foundation which is God to build your marriage on so that it will work. God is the same all the time. When God puts two people together it is usually because their gifts work well together to help edify the body of Christ. Men have to hear from God on their wives but if you are not where you suppose to be in God your husband may not be able to find you. He knows what God has for him and if you as a woman still don't know what your purpose and your worth is in Christ then you can miss who God really has for you. Focus on God and stop focusing on a man so he can get you ready to receive what he has for you. Remember that your timing is not God's timing and we should thank God that he is a just God, a forgiving God and that he doesn't act like us. Can you imagine if God treated us like we treat him? We need to realize that he is just not our God but he should be our Lord and he should rule over every part of our lives. We need to wait on God so that it will be right and not wrong.

Reflections: How will you change how you wait until God send you his chosen mate?

12.
The Married Woman

The married woman must carry herself different than a single woman. Married women should be selective of who they talk with about their marriage. **(Rip) Stop expecting your single friends to help you with your marriage!** Ladies, they can't help you fix yours when they are trying to get themselves in order for their husbands to find them. **(Tip) If you cannot work it out with your husband then seek professional counseling from someone you can trust and know the word of God.** There is no I, me or mine in a real relationship. Those have to be replaced with we, us and ours. I don't know where the saying comes from that we should be 50/50 in a relationship. In order for it to work both parties have to be willing to give 100/100 percent because 99 percent will just not do. God doesn't want us to give him half of us he wants all of us, therefore we must be willing to put all parts of us in so that our marriage will benefit. There should always be open communication with one another and complete honesty with each other. **(Rip) Ladies, you cannot want him to give you all of him when you are not ready to give him all of you.** That means the good, bad and the ugly. Your husband should also be your best friend. There are so many marriages built on the wrong thing and there is no trust. **(Tip) When you become one, be willing to do just that.** That includes your phone codes, your social media, and the bank accounts. If you are not ready to let your husband in on everything you do, then ladies you are not ready to become one with a man. Decisions need to be made together since they will affect the entire household. Marriage is something you are willing to work on daily because everyday will not be easy. Marriages are not perfect, but God is. The secret to marriage is not a mystery. People make marriage so hard because they are not willing to be open about everything, share and be willing to change things that may not work for your partner. For example, tell your husbands where you are going when you leave the house. Not for control purposes, but for protection. If something should happen to you he will at least know where to start. These secrets that lies in marriages need to stop! Let's keep it simple, the marriage will work as long as the foundation is built on God and that each person is doing their part to please God. Keeping God's commandments will put you in order with your spouse. If God is happy with you then your spouse will be happy with you as well.

Reflections: What ways can you help better your marriage so that you can prevent a miscarriage?

_____
_____
_____
_____
_____

13.
Married Single/Single Married Women

This section can be a little difficult, however there are so many women stuck in this chapter. When you are a wife and have a husband but are doing your role and his role because he isn't where he suppose to be in Christ this is considered to me as a married single woman. You are doing everything on your own because your husband has other agendas that he is focused on and you are not in his plan. You may want to ensure that you are not a married single woman. When you don't have anything together like bank accounts, insurances, cars, and your house is even separate, this needs to be evaluated. Living separate from your mate can give the enemy the room he needs to tempt you. Why marry if you are going to continue to be single? You should pray to your father and evaluate the situation. In most of these cases the Lord has already given you your answer and you have already realized that you did not wait on God for your husband or you have decided because you have been in it for so long you might as well stay. We get that you are trying to honor the vows however is this the plan God had or did you pick your husband in the first place? I heard a wise man of God say that "the hardest places to be is the ones that God didn't want you to be in." We have to stop telling ourselves that this is God's plan when you know that God didn't have anything to do with it. We may have allowed the flesh to override our minds and hearts, but this can't always be the excuse that it is not getting any better. **(Rip) Stop settling for his manhood down there to get you off of God's track up there!** Ladies we know what down there is but up there is your mindset. You don't have to settle for what the world would like you to have in a man but you have the right to have what God has for you, his Godsent man. If you are not getting everything you should be getting in your marriage, then you and your husband should seek counseling and decide whether or not it is working or worth working it. I have gotten sick and tired of seeing so many good women waiting on these men who didn't want to be married in the first place and now the wife is left to deal with it. The Bible is still true that God honors marriages and even though you may be a married-single woman God still covers you because you are not in sin. On the other hand, you have single-married women who has devoted all their good qualities to a man who has never intended to be married in the first place. The Bible does talk about patience being a virtue, **(Rip) However, it is a big difference between patience and stupidity! (Tip) Women, we should be patient and wait on God to send us our husband and even wait on when he is ready to move to the next step.** Stupidity on the hand is when you picked your own man and has been dating him over some decades and he still hasn't married you yet. The saying, "why buy the cow when you get the milk for free" is so true. Ladies, be careful of these men who just want a girlfriend for a long time because he's too much of a coward for commitment. **(Tip) A man**

knows whether he wants to marry you or not after the first year, but he will stay around for all the free goodies. Man has gotten used to us allowing them to have their cake and eat it too while we are waiting to be a wife. He's happy that he gets everything like a wife, but he has no intentions of supporting you later as his wife. We as women must not settle for this. If he doesn't want to marry you and make you his wife, then he is not worthy of the benefits you are giving him on the intentions of him becoming your husband. The Lord didn't intend for us as women to be a girlfriend forever. God was very specific when he made the word and one commandment said not to fornicate or commit adultery. Women, if you are a woman scared of commitment and you think it is easier to date someone else's husband because you like the benefits with no attachment then you are not living according to God's word either. In the Old Testament, the Bible states, "and the man that committeth adultery with another man's wife, even he that committeth adultery with his neighbor's wife, the adulterer and the adulteress shall surely be put to death (Lev 20:10)." Also in the new testament it states, "but I say unto you, that whosoever looketh on a woman to lust after her hath committed adultery with her already in his heart (Matt.5:28)." **(Rip) While you think it is easier to be with someone else's man or woman, you are disrespecting God, yourself and showing off your Jezebel or king David's spirit! (Tip) There will always be consequences of breaking God's commandments so you should repent to God, yourself and that other person and wait on what God has for you.** When we allow that man to make us his girlfriend forever, he robs us of an opportunity of being loved by a Godsent man and becoming his wife for life. If you are in a fake marriage because you are still single after decades, then you must step up to your feelings and that boy and tell him that you desire to be a wife and not a boy toy. This could mean a possibility of being without him, but he has worn his welcome out anyway! You have to protect your heart and your purpose in Christ no matter what. Look back at the relationship to realize that you were making him look good and what has he really done for you lately? Just because he wants to live his life out of the will of Christ doesn't give him the right to choose for you. Just keep it simple, if it is contrary to the word of God then it is not right. If you do choose to stay with him then cut out the wifely benefits and focus on God more so that he can show you who that boy is in the first place. You will find out that he lusted for you but didn't love you. He lusted after what you can do for him but didn't love you enough to make you his wife. Pay attention to all the excuses they have not to marry you. Real men aren't afraid of commitment, they want you to carry their last names. Real men want to support you even after he goes home with the Lord and real men know how to honor their father in heaven and want to make sure he is right in the eyes of the Lord. We must stop being a victim of fake love because you deserve to get all that God has for you and not only what man wants you to have. God wants us to have real love and not worldly lust.

Reflections: What decisions will you have to make

in order to get rid of the fake? Or what will you and your husband talk about to make him know you need him to help out?

14.
A Sanctified Woman

What is sanctified? It is being set apart from the world. So a sanctified woman is saved then set apart from the worldly woman. A woman should always carry herself with dignity, honor and respect. Ladies you should never allow anyone especially a man to take you out of your character of who you are in the Lord. A sanctified woman is set apart from the worldly woman meaning you shouldn't be fast to be ready to get angry or be ready to fight when someone says something you don't like. That is allowing the enemy to take over your spirit. The word says, "Wherefore, my beloved brethren, let every man be swift to hear, slow to speak, slow to wrath: for the wrath of man worketh not the righteousness of God (James 1:19)." That means we have to not be ready to argue but to listen, we have to not say the first thing that comes to our mind and not be ready to fight or get out of our characters. Ladies, be wise of the words that you say to hurt because once they come out you can't take them back. Even if you apologize or give apolo-lies, words hurt and they can tear people down. Ladies, sometimes our emotions want to speak first so that the person can feel hurt like we do, but trying to hurt people only shows that you need to deal with the hurt inside of you. It doesn't make you better because you feel that you won the argument. It should make you feel worse because you failed the test of being set apart from the world and that some of your hurt is not healed. Ladies again I say that if it hurts, deal with it. You need to ask God for forgiveness, ask that person for forgiveness and leave it alone so that your healing will start coming. The word says, "Bear with each other and forgive one another if any of you has a grievance against someone. Forgive as the Lord forgives you (Colossians 3:13)." You cannot move on with unforgiveness in your heart because it holds up your blessings from the Lord. Unforgiveness can also cause sickness in our bodies so let it go because forgiveness is for you and not the other person. This is why we need to control our sharp tongues because the word says, "That death and life is in the power of the tongue: and they that love it shall eat the fruit thereof (Proverbs 18:21)." So again I say read and study your word so that you can be better equipped to deal with the everyday struggles that will come.

Reflections: How will you be set apart which allows God to stay in your heart?

_____

_____

_____

_____

_____

_____

_____

_____

_____

15.
The Virtuous Woman

Ladies, we need to be like the woman in the Bible who was talked about in the word. Proverbs chapter 31 talks about what a good woman is. This woman knows how to work, provide for her family and support her husband. It mentioned how she was clothed with strength and dignity. Women, have we lost our dignity? Why have we let all of our morals down to please the wrong type man? The best thing about this woman is that she fears the Lord. The scripture says, "Charm is deceptive, and beauty is fleeting; but a woman who fears the Lord is to be praised (Proverbs 31:30)." **(Rip) Ladies stop focusing on your beauty, giving up the booty and rise up to your duty. (Tip) Your duty is to honor and fear God so that you can get your praise from your father above.** Remember that if you are making your father in heaven pleased with you, that man should also be pleased with you. If he is not, then he is not the right one. There is so much work that needs to be done in the body of Christ so you should not be using idle time to be looking for a man because it is not biblical. The only thing you should be doing is seeking for more of the Lord and praying that God will show you what your gifts are and how they need to be used in the body of Christ. If and when you become a wife you need to make sure that you are building him up and not tearing him down, that you are supporting him even when you don't think he is making the right decision, that you are praying for him to be closer to God so that your entire house is protected, that you are working alongside his gifts and talents so that he is better, when he is not at his best you nurture him back to his best. Through good and bad, better or worse, sickness and health, richer or poor you must be there and willing to be his helpmate at all times so that you are honored by God and him. You have to be faithful at all times and looking your best so that he will shine. Ladies, you can't be selfish and when you're tired of him you want to cheat or have an affair. **(Rip) How are you going to be faithful to man and you are cheating on God!** You are in the word one minute and in the world the next minute. You give God five minutes but you talk to the worldly man five hours. You doubt God and only worship him when he says yes to you. When he tells you no or wait you go out and mess it up yourself then pray that God will fix it for you. It doesn't work like that. **(Tip) You can't be a hot mess hello and then want God to make it go away bye-bye! (Tip) Virtuous women don't put all their business on social media to gain attention, hurt women do.** When you are trying to get validation and pity parties from social media network this is a dead giveaway that you need to change something about you. Your business is your business and everyone doesn't need to know it. There are too many miserable people who want company. Stay away from negative attention and so-called friends who want to always be involved in drama. Social media should not be getting more of your time than God. I challenge you to give God at least the same time you give social media and television and I guarantee that your life will change. I am calling all women to your virtuous spot so that we are pleasing in God's eyes. Single women be strong and learn to carry yourself as a virtuous women now so that you will already know how to be one when God sends you your Godly man.

Reflections: What qualities of virtue do you have or want to have so that the wrong man cant hurt you?

16.
Give God More

Women, we have to be ready to give God more than what we have been given. We expect God to give us so much, everything we pray for and the finest man with all the benefits, but we are not willing to put in the work in getting any of this. **(Rip) Stop expecting God to fix your mess when you are only striving to give God less!!** First of all, we go out and get the man that we feel that we need because the outside looks right to the flesh. Oh yes ladies he's tall, dark skin, handsome, thuggish and he got money but in the inside he has a predator mentality and wants to eat your flesh, kill your spirit and move on to the next. **(Tip) We have to stop allowing ourselves to be the prey.** There is a saying that women have an intuition and I am going to call it discernment. You will see some signs that something isn't right and even feel it in your spirit that it is too good to be true but because it looks good, feels good and the lifestyle is right we will settle for the disrespect of him cheating on you, cursing you out and even putting his hands on you while you are left justifying his bad behaviors to your family and friends. You are even okay with disobeying the word of God knowing that he is not saved and not thinking about being saved. The Bible says, "Be ye not unequally yoked together with unbelievers: for what fellowship hath righteousness with unrighteousness? And what communion hath light with darkness (2 Corinthians 6:14)?" It is not God's plan for you to be unhappy with a person who doesn't believe in the God you serve and want to control and abuse you like you mean nothing to him. The Bible talks about what love is and what love is not. The Bible says, "Love is patient, love is kind. It does not envy, it does not boast, it is not proud. It does not dishonor others, it is not self-seeking, it is not easily angered, it keeps no record of wrongs. Love does not delight in evil but rejoices with the truth. It always protects, always trusts, always hopes, always perseveres (1 Cor 13:4-6)." **(Tip) Love doesn't beat you down, bring your self-esteem down, so his can be up, call you out of your character and use you only to get what he want so he can boast later with his friends!** These qualities are contrary to the word of God. We must really start reading our word, understanding it and getting wisdom so that we can apply it to our everyday lives. Again we perish for a lack of knowledge so now that you have it how will you use it? We intend to make the devil responsible for everything that goes wrong in our lives but let's be real, sometimes it's you. You wanted that man so God may have allowed his permissive will for your life and not his perfect will. The saying be careful what you pray for because you might just get it. We have to be careful not to pray for things that we are not ready for. This could be hurtful to our spirit and our lifestyles. We have to give God more so that our spirits can get stronger and that we will die daily to our flesh. Our flesh is a mess, but God wants our spirit at its best. We have to realize that God is not in a box. The minute we take him out the box the word say, "Now unto him that is able to do exceeding abundantly above all that we ask or think, according to the power that worketh in us (Ephesians 3:20)." Ladies what are you asking for and where is your power? God even said think meaning he will bless us with things that we haven't even thought about. This shows us again that God is not in a box, but we are and we are trapped because we are not wise to know that we have the power to get out of it. **(Tip) The man God may have for you may not look like the ones that you have always dated or who you think you need.** He may not have the money you think you need. Maybe the problem is that you need to allow yourself to date out of the norm. A God man may not have the looks, but he has the heart of God who can love you like nobody else. He might not have the physique of a bodybuilder, but he understands that he is physically involved in the word of God, and is geared with the armor of God so that he can stand against the wiles of the enemy. He may not be rich, but he is rich in the knowledge of God and understand his worth in God's kingdom. Once we get our hands out of helping God help us, we will understand that God doesn't need our help. We mess it up all the time which causes God to have to fix it and make it right. Try giving God more in his word, in your prayers and in your body of Christ so that you can get what God really has for you. You should eventually get tired of doing the same thing over and over and expecting a different result which is just the definition of being insane. The Webster dictionary says, insane is being mentally ill. We need to stop acting insane because that is not God's way. It is time we make a stand and show the male the reason why God made us in the beginning. We're suppose to walk beside the man and not behind him or under his foot. God loves order and if he wanted us to be in the back he would have made us from Adam's back and if he wanted us to be stepped on then we would have been made from man's feet. Stop allowing men to treat you like you are not their helpmates and that they don't need you at all.

Reflections: How will you overcome to the flesh less and trust God more to be at your best?

_____
_____
_____
_____
_____
_____
_____
_____
_____
_____
_____
_____
_____
_____

17.
Get You a Bible-Based Church

Church is just not the building; church should be a safe place to grow in God. Church should be your family, friends, where you learn from other's mistakes and where you can be corrected in love to get back on track with the Lord. Hearing others testimonies can give you hope and teach you lifelong lessons to help in other parts of your life. It is a trick of the enemy that you don't need to go to church to make it in this difficult life. The Bible says, "Not forsaking the assembling of ourselves together, as the manner of some is; but exhorting one another: and so much the more, as ye see the day approaching (Hebrews 10:25)." Then Jesus said, "For where two or three are gathered together in my name, there am I in the midst of them (Matthew 18:20)." I am not saying that the church is not in your heart but I am saying that you will not get the same experience at home that you will around other sisters who can help pray for you. We have to really stop punishing God for being church hurt. There are so many people who have so many reasons why they don't go to church. No matter if you was hurt, or the leaders weren't following God or you were only at the church because of family or a past relationship that went left God didn't change or do anything to wrong you. It is a trick of the enemy that now you feel all churches are the same and it is not for you. **(Rip) Remembering all**

those excuses is because you just don't want to go! If you are not going to church because of what happened in the church, then you were going for them and not him. **(Tip) The church is where we come when we are spiritually sick and need healing so you cannot stop going because someone else is sick.** We continue to go to the doctor when we are sick to get healing so what is the difference? We should have our own relationship with the Lord meaning you should know the Bible for yourself. You shouldn't be putting your faith in man because it will fail you every time but putting your faith in God is the best foundation you could ever have. If you don't have a church and you are in the East Spencer area come get you some New Life at New Life Community Church where the pastor will not sugarcoat the word of God and the ladies there will encourage, support and pray you through when you need them the most. Come to a place that not only cares about your soul but cares about helping you with building your self-confidence with a God giving confidence statement that the pastor has written and included in the everyday service. The leaders are not just teaching the word but they are living the word every day in their personal lives as well. Remember that we are spirits with a flesh and not a flesh with a spirit meaning we should feed our spirits with the spirit of God and die to our flesh daily. We should be working in our home church and not just being a looker. **(Rip) There are too many lazy people in the body of Christ who have so much they can offer to edify the body but would rather be a spectator and then have the nerve to talk about the ones who are working.**

(Tip) We need to stop being religious and get a relationship with God. The enemy doesn't care about your title and how many scriptures you can quote, because he knows that as long as he can keep you living like the world, he still got you. Be careful of wanting titles that you are not ready for because if you claim it the enemy will attack you on that level. We should just focus on serving and doing that the best you can to Christ. Whatever you do we should do it to God which should be in excellence. We should focus on loving one another and being thankful that God wants our reasonable service.

Reflections: Are you in the right ministry where your leader cares about your soul and not your money and your role?

_____
_____
_____
_____
_____
_____
_____
_____
_____
_____
_____
_____

18.
Iron Sharpens Iron

Ladies, I am glad that you have pushed yourself to deal with your own flaws while getting the empowerment that you need. Remember that you are not the minority, you are the majority. We should encourage and always be there to help one another. Don't be jealous of other's blessings but celebrate with them. God knows that you are ready for your blessings when you can celebrate with someone else in their blessings. Women, you are beautiful individuals inside and out, but you have to make sure that people can see the right type of beauty. Beauty is a lot more than what you can see on the outside, but beauty starts in the inside with your heart. You are smart and nurturing and that is why the enemy will try to play on your emotions. We can't let our emotions take control all the time because they will act on your flesh. You are needed to make this world go around and that is why you have to find your purpose in Christ so that you can help someone else. Women, you are blessed and favored by God and that is why the scripture says, "He who finds a wife finds what is good and receives favor from the Lord (Proverbs 18:22)." Your Godsent man is looking and he cannot get favor without you. You are necessary and that is why there are three of us to one man. You are resilient. Women are one of the strongest creatures God created and that is why we can handle childbirth and female problems on a daily basis. Even though we caused the fall of man God extended his grace and mercy for us to still have a purpose in him, so we have to use our position to honor the Lord. Women, you are loved by God no matter what your situation looks like or the cards you were dealt. God knew you and chose you and he wants the total you. Just because it happened to you and it hurt, God will turn that hurt into healing causing you to admit that it happened for a reason. God can turn shame into fame so that you can be rich in him. God can turn rape into shape and mold you into the woman he wants you to be. God can turn hurt into alert so that you are aware of when the enemy is trying to attack you. God will do exactly what he said he would do because he is omnipotent, meaning he has unlimited power and can do anything. So when you get down and feel like nobody understands, talk with the almighty God who made you, who knows how many hair particles you have on your head and knows your next steps so that he can give you guidance. We have to be able to use the scriptures to empower ourselves so get your scriptures so that when anything comes to bring you down you can counteract it with the word of God. We should not leave the house without putting on the whole armor of God which is the breastplate of righteousness, feet filled with readiness of peace, the shield of faith, helmet of salvation and the sword of the spirit which is the word of God and be ready to pray in the spirit (Ephesians 6:11-13). We can't afford to have some of it on and not all of it because the part that is not on is where the enemy will try to attack you. Study your word daily so that you can look and be more like the Lord. If you are single and waiting for your man to find you, get closer to God so that you will not be ruined by the wrong man. The stronger you are in God the better you will be when he comes. If you are married already, pray and have your own relationship with the Lord. Pray daily for you and your spouse and pray with your spouse as well. Stay on one accord and don't let anyone come between the union you have with the Lord and your husband. The word says, "They are no longer two, but one. Therefore, what God has joined together, let no man separate (Matthews 19:6)." Lean on each other because both of you are stronger together. If you are married and are having issues, pray about it and it is ok to get Christian counseling from someone that both of you trust. "There is nothing too hard for God (Jeremiah 32:17)." Time is getting short and it is not time to play with the Lord. Be strong, true to God and yourself so that you can change yourself and stop trying to change the man. I love each one of you and I hope that something was said that can help you to get a closer relationship with the Lord so that he can help with your inner and outer you. Please share this book with everyone that you feel that needs it and I can't wait to hear your success stories on how you were able to build yourself and deny temptation from the enemies who don't want to see you better. I made this book for you so that you can reference it when you are in a hard place. Keep the word of God in your heart and this book in your car to let it be a quick reference guide. **(THIS IS NOT A REPLACEMENT FOR THE BIBLE BUT A PATHWAY FOR YOU TO WANT TO READ THE WORD MORE.)** I love you my sisters and God loves us too. Blessings to you and your family and please share it with everyone man or woman you know and even with a group of women for discussion. Be on the lookout for Rips, Tips and Scripts Part 2 and Struggles of a Good Wife. If you haven't read A Scary Life to a Loving Wife please support me. Please reach out to me by email if you should have any questions or want me to come help you explain it better. Email me at keatontamelia@gmail.com.

Reflections: How can you tell your story to be able to help lead someone else to their glory? Also share how you turned your hot mess into a God bless.

_____
_____
_____
_____
_____
_____
_____
_____
_____
_____
_____
_____
_____

About the Author

My name is Tamelia Keaton known as Mia. I was born in Winston-Salem, NC and have been residing here all my life. I am married to Miguel Keaton who is a disabled veteran. Together we have five sons and one bonus son. I am a person who loves traveling to see different places with my family, Zumba with my Zumba family, hanging out with my church family and writing in my spare time. I went to Carver High School where I obtained my diploma and enjoyed running track. I obtained my Bachelor's degree graduating Cum Laude in Healthcare Management with a specialization in Gerontology from American Intercontinental University in Atlanta Georgia. As I pursued my studies, I pledged to be a part of Alpha Sigma Lambda, and the Honors Society club as well. I have had a long career with Food Lion having the pleasure to be a Customer Service Manager and Front End Manager. I have also had the honor of working for Wells Fargo Bank where I experienced every role in retail banking and advanced to become a Branch Manager at one of the locations in Winston-Salem. I now enjoy caregiving with private clients and supporting my own family. I enjoy motivating others to bring out their boldness and discovering their purpose for the body of Christ. I am a person who loves to serve wherever my skills are needed.

Made in the USA
Middletown, DE
04 June 2025